ROSES

The Gardener's Collection

Better Homes and Gardens® Books

Des Moines

MEREDITH® BOOKS
President, Book Group: Joseph J. Ward
Vice President and Editorial Director: Elizabeth P. Rice
Art Director: Ernest Shelton

ROSES
Senior Editor: Marsha Jahns
Editor: Cathy Howard
Art Director: Michael Burns
Copy Editors: Durrae Johanek, Kay Sanders, David Walsh
Assistant Editor: Jennifer Weir
Administrative Assistant: Carla Horner
Special thanks: Ann Reilly

MEREDITH CORPORATION CORPORATE OFFICERS:
Chairman of the Executive Committee: E. T. Meredith III
**Chairman of the Board, President
and Chief Executive Officer:** Jack D. Rehm
Group Presidents:
   Joseph J. Ward, Books
   William T. Kerr, Magazines
   Philip A. Jones, Broadcasting
   Allen L. Sabbag, Real Estate
Vice Presidents:
   Leo R. Armatis, Corporate Relations
   Thomas G. Fisher, General Counsel and Secretary
   Larry D. Hartsook, Finance
   Michael A. Sell, Treasurer
   Kathleen J. Zehr, Controller and Assistant Secretary

*All of us at Meredith® Books are dedicated to providing you
with the information and ideas you need to garden
successfully. We guarantee your satisfaction with this book for
as long as you own it. If you have any questions, comments,
or suggestions, please write to us at:*

MEREDITH®BOOKS, Garden Books
Editorial Department, RW 240
1716 Locust St.,
Des Moines, IA 50309-3023

*T*hroughout history, no one flower has been more cherished, revered, or steeped in tradition than the rose. An old-fashioned symbol of love, roses profusely repay a gardener's devotion with their beauty, fragrance, and graceful form.

CONTENTS

TYPES OF ROSES 6

ROSES IN THE LANDSCAPE 20

ROSE CARE AND MAINTENANCE 28

DIRECTORY OF ROSES 44

INDEX 64

Types of Roses

*F*ossils prove that roses grew millions of years ago. Today, with more than 12,000 varieties in her court, this monarch among flowers remains a favorite in people's hearts and gardens. One reason is the rose's versatility. Available in a dizzying array of colors, heights, fragrances, and forms, roses are as fascinating as they are lovely.

Old Garden Roses

From the antique varieties to the aristocratic hybrid tea, roses form a robust family of many types. There are vigorous climbers that frame an entire arbor and charming miniatures that can grow daintily in a teacup. For centuries, rose growers have experimented with creating new varieties. As a result, there are thousands of roses from which to choose.

Lowest-maintenance roses include old garden roses, shrub roses, and species roses. Hybrid teas, floribundas, grandifloras, shrub roses, and miniatures are especially long-flowering.

For bedding and formal borders, plant floribundas or hybrid teas. The new English roses of David Austin and the French Meidiland roses offer long bloom and hardiness, and are ideal in many landscape settings. Climbers, tree roses, and miniature roses provide profuse bloom for special spots in the garden, from containers to arbors.

Old Garden Roses An old garden rose is any rose that predates the introduction of the hybrid tea in 1867. These old varieties developed from five original European "families" that bloomed just once each year, in May or June.

Old roses are often pink or red, with a loose, untamed look compared with the tight-budded hybrid teas. The roses are prized for their bounty of fragrant blooms, easy care, charm, long life, and differing flower forms and colors. Most are hardy in winter, are disease and pest resistant, and require little maintenance.

Revered for generations, antique roses have retained the unique qualities that made them popular in days past. The hardiest roses in this class are the older varieties that bloom only once: albas, damasks, gallicas, and moss roses. Wild or species roses also are considered old garden roses. Two other antique roses came to Europe from Asia—China and tea roses—and became ancestors of the modern hybrids.

Albas are tall, dense, disease resistant, and covered with clusters of fragrant white or pink blooms. They bloom only once a year but are worth the wait.

Bourbons reward you with blooms throughout the season. Plants are moderately hardy, vigorous, and have clusters of fragrant double flowers.

Centifolias are called cabbage roses because they have 100 or more overlapping petals; they also are called Provence roses for the section of France where they were once widely grown. Their globular, fragrant flowers, white to deep rose, bloom once a year on slender, arching branches.

White 'Sombreuil,' red 'Crimson Glory,' and pink 'Aloha' climbing roses grace the railings of this front porch.

Damasks are known for their fragrance. Except for autumn damasks, they bloom only once. Flowers are medium to large on drooping, arching branches. They are extremely hardy and disease resistant.

Gallicas, a French rose cultivated since the 13th century, blooms once in spring with single or double pink, red, or purple flowers. Called the Apothecary's Rose because of its many medicinal uses, it produces edible rose hips in the fall.

Old Garden Roses

Moss roses first appeared in the early 1700s as mutations, or sports, of centifolias and damasks. Recognizable by the hairy glands on bud and foliage, these roses were popular with Victorian gardeners. Moss roses bloom slightly later in the spring than other types.

Hybrid perpetuals are the link between old and modern roses, with single or double roses blooming repeatedly throughout the season. They are tall, vigorous, and hardy. Hybrid rugosas are rugged shrubs derived from *Rosa rugosa*.

Hybrid spinosissimas are modern additions to the shrub border. They are valued for their bloom.

Noisettes are good climbers for mild areas, producing clusters of blooms in white, pink, red, purple, and yellow throughout the summer. They can grow with Portlands, which are sturdy, erect bushes with double, fragrant flowers. Both bloom all summer.

Species or wild roses are robust native roses with single flowers. Some bloom only once; others bloom repeatedly.

China roses have delicate, repeating flowers and, like pastel tea roses, played an important role in the development of modern roses because of their repeat bloom. Both China and tea roses aresensitive to the cold. Mildew-resistant Chinas are pink or red; tea roses are similar in growth habit, with large cupped blooms that smell like green tea leaves.

Favorite antique roses include 'Celestial' (alba), 'Fantin Latour' (centifolia), 'Madame Hardy' (damask), 'Charles de Mills' and 'Rosa Mundi' (gallicas), and 'Blanche Moreau' (moss).

Alba 'Queen of Denmark'

Gallica 'Charles de Mills'

Modern Roses

A chance crossing of a hybrid perpetual with a tea rose in 1867 produced the first modern rose, 'La France.' This new rose, a hybrid tea, had neat growing habits and bloomed often—characteristics it inherited from the tea rose. And like the hybrid perpetual, it was hardy in winter. A wave of hybridizing followed and continues still today.

Hybrid tea roses define the classic beauty of today's roses. As long, pointed buds open, they reveal swirls of petals and high-centered, elegant blooms in every color but blue. Many of the plants, which grow 2 to 5 feet tall, emit the fine and famous rose fragrance. Alone or in arrangements, hybrid teas are perfect for bringing indoors as cut flowers on long stems.

Some hybrid teas are hardy; most, however, require special care where winters are severe.

To please Victorian tastes, hybrid teas were bred for large blossoms, heady fragrance, and perpetual flowering, along with the famed barely open bloom that has made them the aristocrat of cut flowers. Favorites include 'Chrysler Imperial,' 'Mister Lincoln,' 'Peace,' and 'Tropicana.'

Floribundas produce abundant clusters of flowers with several open at once. Created by crossing the hybrid tea with the shrubby polyantha, floribundas are larger, bushier, hardier, and more disease and mildew resistant than hybrid teas. They are the perfect landscape rose, with sprays of flowers in bloom nearly all season.

Bushy and compact, floribundas are ideal for hedges, borders, and mass plantings. Favorites include 'Iceberg,' 'Simplicity,' 'Sun Flare,' and 'Vogue.'

Polyanthas, which developed almost simultaneously with the hybrid tea, are a cross between *Rosa multiflora* and *Rosa chinensis.* The roses in this class have low-growing plants smothered with clusters of 1-inch flowers. Polyanthas widely grown today

Floribunda 'Sunsprite'

include classics such as 'The Fairy,' 'China Doll,' and 'Cécile Brünner'— all with pink flowers. Other popular polyanthas include a group of roses in shades of orange and red that are named for the famous Koster family of rose hybridizers, and 'Polyantha Grandiflora,' a white rose with the scent of oranges.

Modern Roses

Grandifloras were created in 1954 with the introduction of the rose 'Queen Elizabeth.' They exhibit the best traits of their parents: the flower form and long cutting stem of the hybrid tea and the hardiness, continuous flowering, and clustering of the floribunda. Usually tall, they are more vigorous than either parent. Grandifloras often are planted as a backdrop for other roses, as a screen, or as a source for cut flowers.

Favorites in this group include 'White Lightnin',' 'Gold Medal,' 'Queen Elizabeth,' and 'Sonia.'

Shrub roses are appropriate for any landscape setting or border, providing color longer than most shrubs. They vary in size from low-growing ground covers such as 'Max Graf' and 'Sea Foam' to tall plants like 'Dortmund.' Other well-known varieties include 'Golden Wings,' 'Sparrieshoop,' and 'Bonica.'

Most shrub roses are disease resistant and require little maintenance. They tolerate neglect and poor growing conditions and are easy to prune. Shrub rose categories include hybrid musk roses and *Rosa rugosa.*

Developed in the 20th century, hybrid musk shrub roses boast a heavy fragrance and a long flowering period. The roses have pliable canes that can be trained along a low fence or wall. Varieties are shade tolerant, disease resistant, and moderately hardy.

The classic *Rosa rugosa* shrub rose gets its name from the wrinkled, or "rugose," texture of its bright green foliage. A favorite of many gardeners who once swore off roses, this rugged type thrives even in poor soils and extreme weather. As shrubs or hedges, rugosas bloom almost constantly from spring through summer and

Gardener's Tip

Give roses an insulating blanket of mulch for their winter nap. Move container-grown roses to a garage or porch and cover the crowns with straw.

Shrub rose 'All That Jazz'

Shrub rose 'Bonica'

develop colorful, edible fruit, or hips, in the fall. Pruning is optional.

Favorite shrub roses include 'Felicia' and 'Penelope' (hybrid musks), 'Little White Pet' (polyantha), 'Blanc Double de Coubert' and 'Rosa Rugosa Scabrosa' (rugosas), 'Red Blanket' (ground cover), and 'Golden Wings' (modern shrub).

Modern Roses

Climbing roses capture the poetry of a summer garden, whether draped over an arch, rambling along a fence, or twined about a post. There are two types: ramblers and climbers.

Ramblers have long, pliable stems that bear huge clusters of tiny flowers once in late summer. Train these plants on open structures, not walls, because they are mildew-prone.

Climbers have stiffer stems, bear larger flowers, and may bloom more than once a year. Plants form a dense screen on a fence, wall, or trellis. Climbers are also easier to prune and maintain than ramblers. Without the tendrils that vines have, these tall roses need to be trained and tied to a support.

Ramblers primarily are offspring of *Rosa wichuraiana* and *Rosa multiflora,* and are huge, fast growers. They tolerate cold northern latitudes better than some climbers.

Favorites include ramblers 'Albertine,' 'Wedding Day,' and 'Emily Gray' and climbers 'City of York,' 'Danse du Feu,' 'Cécile Brünner,' 'Handel,' 'Swan Lake,' 'Blaze,' 'White Dawn,' and 'Compassion.'

Miniature roses, favored for their petite delicacy, perform just as their larger cousins do. Sturdy and versatile, these small plants have gained a large following because the average garden has shrunk in size. They are found in rock gardens, window boxes, low

Gardener's Tip

Watch for pesky black spot (a fungus disease) on foliage, a predictable problem in summer heat and high humidity. Nip it in the bud by applying fungicide weekly to all roses. Pick off spotted leaves as soon as they appear and destroy them.

hedges, hanging baskets, patio pots, and even indoors.

Miniature roses resemble their larger relatives except for their blossoms, leaves, and stems, which are much smaller. Plants range from 3 to 24 inches tall.

Favorite varieties are 'Baby Masquerade,' 'Rise 'n' Shine,' 'Darling Flame,' 'Fire Princess,' 'Popcorn,' 'Clipper,' and 'Pour Toi.'

Tree roses are artifically produced by grafting the best parts of three roses to create a fourth. The tree rose takes its root stock from one rose, its straight stem from another, and its vigorous flowers and foliage from yet a third.

The final plant is ideal for use in formal gardens or as an accent for an entrance or patio. The tall stem, or standard, brings blooms to eye level, but this makes the rose sensitive to cold and wind. Use tree roses by themselves or underplant with annuals or floribundas for a more informal effect.

Old-fashioned 'Doctor Huey' roses climb the walls of a cottage.

Miniature tree roses are also available. Topping out at about 2 feet tall, these picturesque plants add a touch of elegance to an entry or patio when displayed in a handsome container, or as a focal point planted near an entry or low wall. The small blooms of a miniature rose clustered on a delicate stem are a captivating garden or patio accent.

New Look of Old Roses

Rose lovers today can rejoice in the development of two new varieties of old-fashioned shrub roses with English and French roots. Tailored for American gardens, David Austin and Meidiland roses offer repeat bloom, delicious fragrance, and a tough-as-nails constitution.

David Austin roses, also known as English roses, are a new breed that has been hailed as "the rose of the future." These hybrids developed by renowned English rose breeder David Austin tie the classic look and fragrance of old-fashioned varieties with the disease resistance and repeat bloom character of more modern types.

Available in a palette of colors, heights, and flower types, David Austin roses are fast becoming favorites in American gardens. 'Graham Thomas,' a gleaming golden yellow; 'Gertrude Jekyll,' a standout pink; and 'English Garden,' a creamy yellow-white, are among the many sensational David Austin roses.

Meidiland Roses Bred for disease resistance, Mediland roses offer beauty without bother. From the House of Meilland, France's premier rose breeder, these everblooming hybrids flourish as low hedges or ground covers. Best of all, they are hardy anywhere in the U.S. Varieties include low-growing 'White Meidiland' and 'Scarlet Meidiland,' and 4-foot varieties 'Bonica' and 'Pink Meidiland.'

'White Meidiland' (above). 'Scarlet Meidiland' (opposite)

Roses in the Landscape

*E*very yard has room for at least one rosebush. Consider some of the many ways you can put roses to use in your yard or garden—as a foundation planting; as a border along a fence, a walk, or a vegetable garden; massed for a wall of bloom by a deck; potted up for a spot of color on a patio; or climbing a trellis.

Using Roses

Even the smallest garden becomes spectacular when a breathtaking rose is in bloom.

Uses of roses range as widely as the flowers' colors, shapes, heights, and varieties. Roses can enhance any landscape, whether it's formal or cottage style, large or small. As long as an area is bathed in at least six hours of sunshine a day, you can add allure with roses.

In Containers Pretty and portable in pots, many varieties of roses that grow compactly are ideal for patio, deck, or porch. Miniatures and tree roses are perfect when space is at a premium, in small city gardens, on rooftops, and on balconies.

In Small Spaces Pocket gardens prove you don't need a lot of room to create a charming landscape. Around a light post, at a corner, rimming a patio—any place with a few square feet of soil can be home to a pretty rose underplanted with a few annuals.

Along Stairs Roses call attention to stairs. If the ground is level, plant taller roses at the back. If the ground slopes with the steps, use roses of the same height to create a wave of color.

Combined with Other Plants Roses mix beautifully with a wide array of other types of plants. Intermingling roses with spring-flowering shrubs in a border, for example, results in color from early spring well into fall—much longer than either plant would provide alone. Use tall roses as backdrops to low-growing shrubs, and low-growing roses as edgings in front of taller evergreen shrubs.

Perennials and roses are an irresistible match. Roses bring continuous color all summer as perennials go in and out of bloom. Mix annuals with roses to change the color scheme each year. Add spring-flowering bulbs to bring early color to your rose garden.

Brighten a patio with pots of roses.

Mix roses with annuals and perennials for three seasons of color.

Using Roses

Against Fences Roses and fences seem made for each other. The fence provides support for tall or rambling roses, while the flowers beautify the structure. An unsightly fence can be camouflaged by a summer-long burst of blossoms with an everblooming rose variety. Brighten a retaining wall by planting climbers or ramblers atop and letting them hang down. Peg the canes to the wall to keep them in place.

For climbers or ramblers, use a fence or wall as the backdrop.

Flanking an Entry While adding emphasis to vertical lines, climbers can cover eaves and outline windows or doors. At the same time, they add color to the exterior of the home and soften hard corners. Such tall beauties need annuals, perennials, or shrubs planted underneath. Or, use rosebushes at the foot of vines, such as clematis, to outline an entryway. Low-growing roses are also a good choice in front of climbers such as thunbergia or morning-glory.

Along a Walk Plant roses beside a garden path or walk in a straight line for a formal, sophisticated look, or curved for a casual, informal effect. Set the bushes back far enough from the edge of the beds so they do not entangle passersby—2 feet is a good rule of thumb for most roses. In a border, where shrubs are planted at least two deep, the plants may be of the

Create an inviting entry with an arbor smothered in roses.

same height. Or place a low-grower along the walk, backed by a taller variety.

As a Privacy Screen Several shrubs planted along the edge of a patio create a floral privacy screen. Lovely on both sides, a thick hedge rose provides color, fragrance, and privacy. Roses intended for screens should be planted closer together than normal to ensure dense, heavily flowered growth.

Between sections of your property or on the property line, roses can substitute for a fence. Plant the bushes two or three deep in a staggered arrangement, setting them a little closer together than normal for fuller color effect. A tall rose such as 'Simplicity' is a good choice.

Gardener's Tip

Every yard has an eyesore. Use roses to camouflage trash cans, sheds, and compost areas.

On Arbors or Trellises Breezy and romantic, a rose arbor is a visual feast for the eye. A rose arbor also adds a bit of shade to a sunny garden. Use climbers on a trellis to accent or camouflage a wall, outline windows, and create a stunning focal point behind other flowers or shrubs.

On Bare Slopes Choose sprawling, low-growing varieties such as 'Max Graf,' 'Red Cascade,' 'White Meidiland,' or 'Scarlet Meidiland' to cover bare slopes or other areas that call for a ground cover. An easy-care mat of summer-long blossom will turn a problem area into a colorful carpet of flowers.

Along a Driveway Planting roses at the entrance to your driveway welcomes visitors with color and fragrance. If the roses are white or pastel, they will stand out at night to mark the entry.

A border of roses and other flowers along a walk or driveway adds instant appeal.

Rose Care and Maintenance

*R*ose plants can survive with minimal care—only water is absolutely necessary— but to obtain the blooms that inspire poets, treat your roses to proper planting, mulching, pruning, feeding, and winter protection.

Planting Roses

Dreams of rose-filled summers start as soon as plant catalogs appear. Soon after, garden centers stock bare-root and container-grown bushes.

Whether you order your rosebushes from a catalog or select them from a garden center is up to you. With a catalog, you're more likely to get the variety you want. With a garden center, you can procrastinate a bit into the season, but the selection may be limited.

Selecting a Site Think carefully about where to put your roses. Their final home should receive at least six hours of full sun a day, preferably in the morning. This allows foliage to dry, reducing the chances of disease. Roses will do best where they'll get light shade in the afternoon. When possible, don't plant roses where their roots will compete with roots from trees and shrubs.

Minatures and climbers will be happy with a little less sun than their larger cousins. High winds can damage or destroy open flowers, so protect roses from wind. Plant them by a fence, hedge, or other barrier.

When to Plant Bare-root roses can be planted in late winter in warm areas. If temperatures don't fall below zero degrees Fahrenheit, planting may be done in early spring or late fall. Where temperatures drop lower, plant only in spring. Container roses can be planted when purchased in summer, allowing you to fill in the garden.

How to Plant Before planting, soak roots of bare-root roses in water overnight to restore lost moisture. Prune back any broken, damaged, or too-long roots.

Dig a hole 24 inches deep and wide, and place a mound of soil in the bottom of the hole. Position the bud union so that it is in line with ground level. Backfill the planting hole two-thirds full, add water, and allow to drain. Fill the hole, then mound soil around the canes to keep them moist. Create a well around the mound and keep it watered.

Roses can be further protected from drying out with a mulch of organic matter. Keep mulch in place until new growth begins, then carefully wash it away with a gentle stream of water.

Prune roses back by a third after planting, and remove any dead or broken wood at the same time. This will encourage new, strong canes to develop.

A variety label is attached with wire to a cane of your new rose. Insert the label in the ground near the rose and keep a record of its growth.

Plan before planting roses in your yard. Place them where they can remain indefinitely.

Spacing Roses Proper spacing of roses varies with the variety. In most climates, 2 feet between hybrid teas, grandifloras, or floribundas will be just right. Where winters are mild, allow more space; for dense edging or hedging, place them a little closer together.

Shrub and old garden roses will grow larger than modern varieties. They are best spaced 4 to 6 feet apart, depending on their mature size. Climbers to be trained horizontally along a fence need 8 to 10 feet between plants. Plant miniature roses from 8 to 18 inches apart, depending on their mature size.

Caring for Roses

If you take care of your roses, they will reward you all summer with beautiful blooms. Proper watering, mulching, fertilizing, and winter protection will help roses survive and flourish.

Soil A rose is no better than the soil in which it's planted, so give extra attention to soil preparation. Soil should be light and rich; improve it by mixing in organic matter, such as peat moss, leaf mold, or compost. Loosen heavy clay soils with gypsum. Because roses don't like wet feet, improve soil drainage by adding vermiculite, perlite, or sand.

Roses appreciate a slightly acid soil—6.0 to 6.5. A soil test will tell if sulfur is needed to make it more acidic or if lime is needed to lower the acidity. Mix superphosphate into the soil for healthy root growth.

Weeding Always keep your rose garden free of weeds. Weeds compete with rose plants for water and food, are breeding grounds for insects and diseases, and are unattractive. Remove weeds as soon as they appear.

Mulch will cut down on weed growth, but when weeds get out of control, step in with careful hand weeding and light hoeing to avoid damaging the roots.

A preemergent chemical herbicide can be applied in the winter. It should be used only after a few killing frosts when temperatures dip below freezing. Keep the herbicide at least a foot away from young rose plants.

Mulching Mulch is a versatile, valuable garden aid. It can be a layer of nearly any material spread on top of the soil to keep it cool, conserve moisture, eliminate weeding, and in some cases, enrich the soil as it decomposes.

Mulches include wood chips, chopped leaves, pine needles, compost, sawdust, or cocoa bean shells. Avoid grass clippings, straw, and hay that contain weed seeds.

Feeding Use a prepared rose food or a balanced fertilizer like 5-10-5. Feed roses at least three times a year: immediately after pruning, after the first bloom cycle, and two months before the first fall frost. To grow larger flowers, fertilize roses once a month during the growing season.

To cut roses or remove spent blooms, make cuts at 45-degree angles above strong, five-leaflet leaves.

Spread fertilizer evenly over moistened soil according to label directions. Lightly work it into the top of the soil or mulch, and water well.

If you use liquid fertilizers only, apply them every two weeks because they leach from the soil quickly. Apply them to the foliage only if the temperature is below 90 degrees.

Remove all side flower buds as soon as they appear on large roses with a single bloom per stem.

Caring for Roses

Watering There are several ways to water your roses: soaker hose, overhead sprinklers, garden hose, or watering can.

A soaker hose conserves water because water trickles from tiny holes punctured along its length. Place a mulch over the soaker hose, and turn the water on to a slow trickle whenever moisture is needed.

Overhead sprinklers keep foliage clean and wash off various insects, but much moisture is lost to evaporation. This type of watering is best done in the morning because wet leaves are prone to disease if they don't dry off quickly. Single rosebushes can be watered by hand or with a hose, wand, or watering can.

Roses need 1 inch of water per week. For best results, water deeply once a week instead of watering lightly more often. If it's hot or windy, or your soil is sandy, water more often.

Seasonal Care Different roses need different amounts of protection where winter temperatures drop below freezing. China, tea, and most pastel hybrid tea, grandiflora, and floribunda roses are tender. Most climbers and miniatures will survive unprotected to zero degrees. Shrub and old garden roses need protection only in areas where temperatures dip to 10 degrees below zero.

Apply winter protection in the fall immediately after the ground freezes. Remove it gradually in the spring, just before pruning. Materials good for winter protection include additional soil, oak leaves, or evergreen boughs.

In the coldest parts of the country, protect roses with plastic-foam cones. Wait until the ground freezes before covering the plants. Most roses will need heavy pruning to fit under the cones. Remove the covers on warm winter days to keep excess heat from stimulating plant growth too early.

You also can make a cylinder of wire mesh to fit around the bush. Gently stuff the cylinder with leaves (don't use maple leaves because they mat down; oak leaves are a good choice). For miniature roses,, simply rake leaves over their tops.

Because tree roses are very tender, bury them, wrap them, or bring them indoors. To bury them, dig up enough of the root system so that you can lay the tree on its side in a trench. Cover with soil. To wrap a tree (see photos at right), set four stakes around the plant. Place burlap around the stakes and secure it. Fill inside the burlap with leaves or shredded newspaper. Where temperatures drop below zero, take climber canes off their supports and secure them to the ground. Cover or wrap the canes.

Propagating Roses Budding is the most widely used commercial method of propagating roses. To try it, home gardeners should buy a special budding knife at a garden shop. In this procedure, buds are removed from a rose and attached to a rose stock, developing a new rose the next spring.

Growing roses from cuttings, either softwood cuttings taken in summer or hardwood cuttings taken in fall, is successful with some species. Roses also can be grown from seed, by layering, or by

Protect tender tree roses from harsh winter weather.

division, depending on the species. Each method poses challenges that may limit the home gardener's success, however.

Pruning Roses

Pruning roses produces vigorous, well-shaped plants full of blooms. Pruning also encourages new canes called basal breaks. Growing from the bottoms of the plants, these canes enable plants to renew themselves year after year.

Proper Tools To do the job properly, buy the right tools. Use pruning shears with curved-edge blades, not the straight-edged anvil variety that can crush stems as they cut.

You also will need long-handled lopping shears to cut out thick branches and prune large shrubs. Keep shears clean and oil them after use. Keep pruning shears sharp, too. Canes with jagged cuts do not heal properly and allow insects and disease to get into the plants.

When to Prune Prune roses in late winter or in early spring, as soon as buds begin to swell but before they start to open. Don't wait until the buds have burst into bright green leaves because then the sap is flowing actively. Somewhere between mid-winter (in the South) and mid-spring (in the North) is the proper time.

Protect yourself from nasty scratches: Pull on a pair of heavy gloves and a long-sleeve shirt. Resist wearing favorite clothing, too; old woody thorns can produce a snag in almost anything.

Pruning Pointers Hybrid teas, floribundas, and grandifloras do well when one-third to one-half of the bush height and width is removed each year. Or trim grandifloras to 18 to 24 inches, and hybrid teas and floribundas to 12 to 18 inches tall.

Keep function in mind, too. For example, if you use floribundas as a hedge, prune them higher and leave on more canes.

For shrub and old garden roses, prune lightly to remove old, weak, or dead wood, or to achieve the desired shape. These roses are best left growing as naturally as possible.

Polyanthas rarely suffer winter damage. In spring, cut their canes back to half their length and remove the oldest canes.

Proper pruning helps ensure large, healthy roses.

Prune miniatures as you would a hybrid tea or floribunda, but on a smaller scale. Cut plants down to 4 to 8 inches, depending on their mature height.

Prune tree roses as you would bush roses, but remember, they are more attractive when symmetrical. Prune all canes to the same length for even growth.

Check the plants several weeks after pruning. A late frost or an unseen canker may have caused one or two canes to die back. Also, make sure you've left no short stubs.

Prune rose plants lightly during their first few years until they become well established and have developed strong canes. To ward off insects that could bore into cut canes, seal cane tips that are more than ½ inch thick with pruning compound or orange shellac.

Pruning Roses

General Pruning When pruning roses, first cut all dead or diseased canes flush with the bud union. Prune any broken or wounded canes or canes with cankers. Prune to below the injuries.

Next, cut out weak canes that are thinner than a pencil. Also remove canes growing into the center of the plant and canes that crisscross. This increases air circulation and discourages diseases. Finally, trim all but three or four of the newest and strongest canes flush with the bud union.

Make all cuts at a 45-degree angle, about ¼ inch above a bud. The cut should slope downward, away from the bud, so water will run off. A cut too close to a bud may kill the bud; a cut too high above a bud may cause the cane to die back. Prune to an outward-facing bud when possible to keep the plant open and nicely shaped.

Pruning Climbing Roses Climbing roses are pruned both early in the spring and after they bloom. Most produce flowers on last year's wood or canes, so they don't need to be pruned as severely as hybrid teas, floribundas, or grandifloras.

Trim dead or broken branches along with overcrowded ones. Pruning more in early spring only results in cutting away the flower buds. However, this is a good time of year to groom the area beneath the plant, raking away debris and applying a mulch to keep weeds down and to conserve moisture.

As bloom time ends, bring out the shears again and remove one or two of the oldest canes. Replacement branches need space to develop properly. Thin the dense growth and small twigs growing from the major cane. Trim any canes that reach beyond their designated space.

A rose plant grows where it is cut, so cut canes back further than you want their final size to be. To get the best bloom, train canes horizontally along a fence, and fasten them several places with plant ties, twine, or rags.

Specialized Rose Pruning Tree roses must be kept symmetrical. Prune canes to a length of 12 inches and leave them evenly spaced around the plant.

Miniatures are pruned according to location. Tiny container-grown plants are pruned as low as 3 inches. Low hedges or edgings are pruned to about 8 inches.

Prune roses in late winter or early spring, as soon as the buds begin to swell, but before they start to open.

Rose Diseases

It takes vigilance to maintain healthy roses. Make regular inspections to catch insects and disease before they can spoil your personal rose festival. Regular feeding, spraying, and dusting will do the job.

The following list includes the most common rose diseases, their symptoms, and methods for controlling the problems.

Black Spot Black spot is a fungus that causes round, black, 1/4-inch spots to appear on the foliage. Eventually a yellow halo forms around each black spot, after which the entire leaf turns yellow and falls off. If your roses had black spot the previous year, prune plants low in spring to remove spores. Water at the soil line to avoid wetting foliage. Use a fungicide as prevention.

Botrytis A fungus that covers buds with a grayish brown, fuzzy growth, botrytis often keeps buds from opening. If buds do open, flowers are flecked with yellow or brown, and petals become brown. Cut out and destroy all infected plant parts. Preventive sprays often are ineffective. The problem is most severe under cool, humid conditions and usually disappears in warmer weather.

Canker Canker is a fungus that enters through a wound and kills the canes. It shows as discoloration on the cane. Chemicals can't control canker; try to prevent wounds. In spring, prune canes below any sign of canker.

Crown Gall Characterized by rough, round growths found around the roots at or below the soil surface, crown gall is a bacterium that stunts growth and reduces flowering.

Prune small galls, disinfecting pruning shears between cuts. In severe cases, discard the plant and the surrounding soil.

Mildew, Downy This type of mildew causes foliage to develop purple to dark brown irregular spots. Leaves turn yellow and eventually fall off. Gray, fuzzy growth may develop on the undersides of leaves. Use a fungicide every seven to 10 days to prevent disease. Discard infected leaves.

Mildew, Powdery A fungus, powdery mildew forms a white powder on buds and leaves. It is most prevalent when nights are cool and days are warm, or where air circulation is poor. Mildew often causes serious disfiguration of the foliage. Improve air circulation around plants and use a fungicide to discourage mildew. Do not water at night. To eradicate, spray with lime-sulfur when the temperature remains below 80 degrees.

Rust is a fungus that forms an orange-red powder on rosebuds, new growth, and leaves. The problem is primarily confined to the West Coast and is caused by mild, wet weather. Inspect new bushes for signs of rust before planting. Destroy a diseased bush.

Spray or dust rose foliage regularly to prevent a variety of diseases.

Control rust on established plants with a fungicide. Remove infected leaves.

Spot Anthracnose Red, brown, or purple spots on upper leaves may indicate spot anthracnose. The centers of the spots eventually turn white, dry, and fall out. Affected leaves turn yellow and fall. Spray with a fungicide every seven days as long as the symptoms persist. Water at soil line.

Rose Insects

Aphids Aphids, or plant lice, are small but visible green, black, red, or brown insects that form colonies along buds and new shoot growth, starting in mid- to late spring. They harm roses by sucking their vital juices. A sticky substance called honeydew may appear on the leaves. Knock aphids off the plant with your fingers or with a strong stream of water from the garden hose, or apply soapy water or a commercial insecticide.

Borers Borers tunnel into canes and under the bark, hollowing out the pith and killing the shoot. Wilting of the plant top may indicate the presence of borers. The cane swells where the borer is hiding. Prune just below each swelling, then apply a sealing compound. Be careful not to injure canes as you work.

Japanese Beetles Japanese beetles are shiny, copper and green insects that can devour an entire garden in a short time. They eat holes in the stems, leaves, and flowers,

particularly white and pastel ones. If the infestation isn't too heavy, use your hands to remove the beetles. For heavy infestations, spray with malathion. Control the grubs in the soil for best results. Spray with malathion.

Leaf-Cutting Bees Leaf-cutting bees cut neat circles into the edges of leaves. The bees do not eat the leaf pieces, but use them to build their nests. Prune severely damaged canes. Because these bees do not eat the foliage, chemicals are ineffective.

Leaf Rollers Green or yellow caterpillars, leaf rollers grow to 1 inch long. They roll themselves up in the rose leaves and eat them from the inside out. Another sign of these pests is tiny holes in the base of the flower buds. Use commercial insecticides or organic controls.

Midges A tiny maggot that bores into roses, midges cause buds, new shoots, and leaves to suddenly blacken and die. To control midges, prune the damage immediately and discard it. Spray insecticide on the tops of plants and apply a systemic insecticide to the ground around the plants.

Nematodes Nematodes are microscopic worms that cause small knotty growths to develop on the roots. Plants lose their vigor. Leaves turn yellow, wilt, and fall. Flowers become smaller. Professional analysis and treatment of the soil may be required. Nematocides are available, but you may need to discard infested plants. Do not plant roses in the same spot for three to four years.

Rose Scales Rose scales are gray, brown, or white hard-shelled insects that encrust stems and suck sap from branches. Plant growth is stunted and flowers don't form. Plants wilt and die. Prune and discard infested canes. Spray with dormant oil in early spring and with commercial systemic insecticide in summer.

Rose Slugs Small, soft, yellow-green caterpillarlike pests, rose slugs start with leaf undersides, then eat the entire foliage, leaving skeletons. They can bore into the pith of pruned canes. Spray with insecticide.

Spider Mites Although it is too small to see, the spider mite's effects are quite obvious. Foliage turns dry and bronze or dull red. In advanced stages, webs can be seen. Technically, it's not an insect, but it does the damage of one.

Since spider mites dislike water, keep plants well watered, and hose down foliage undersides. Apply a miticide three times at three-day intervals.

Thrips Microscopic insects, thrips bore into flowers and suck juices from petals. Buds become distorted and brown, and may not open. Thrips prefer white and pastel roses. They hide in buds and flowers, so cut buds and flowers off and destroy them. Apply an insecticide to the tops of plants.

Directory of Roses

With thousands of varieties of roses available today, deciding which ones to plant can be perplexing. To make the selection process easier, the following pages provide detailed information about many popular roses on the market today.

Hybrid Teas

BARBARA BUSH

Color: Pink/white blend.

Flower Characteristics: Pointed buds open to lightly fragrant 5-inch blooms with 30 to 35 petals. Continuous all-season bloom.

Plant Characteristics: Medium tall. Disease resistant.

Comments: Named to honor the First Lady.

BEWITCHED

Color: Medium pink with yellow stamens.

Flower Characteristics: Large buds open to 5-inch double blooms with 24 to 30 petals. Flowers have a strong rose fragrance and are borne on long, strong, stiff stems. Profuse and continuous all-season bloom.

Plant Characteristics: Medium, upright, and very vigorous.

Comments: An excellent cut flower because of its long vase life and extraordinary scent. All-America Rose Selections (AARS) winner.

BRANDY

Color: Apricot blend with bright golden stamens.

Flower Characteristics: Long, pointed buds open to 5- to 6-inch double blooms with 25 to 30 petals. Flower form is informal and loose. Exhibits a tea fragrance. Blooms profusely all season.

Plant Characteristics: Medium, upright, and vigorous. Disease resistant except for black spot. Winter hardy with some protection.

Comments: Good cut flower because of the classically formed blooms. All-America Rose Selections (AARS) winner.

BRIGADOON

Color: Deep coral pink; lighter pink at base with creamy reverse.

Flower Characteristics: Large, pointed buds open to 5-inch double blooms with 30 to 35 petals. A classic hybrid tea shape, its flowers grow one per stem and bloom abundantly all season.

Plant Characteristics: Medium tall. Very disease resistant.

Comments: Excellent cutting flower because of its unusual color. All-America Rose Selections (AARS) winner.

CHICAGO PEACE

Color: Deep pink with strong yellow at base with some streaks of pink, yellow, and apricot.

Flower Characteristics: Blooms are more than 5 inches wide, very double, and have 50 to 60 petals. Showy, fragrant blooms are even and full form. Good all-season bloom.

Plant Characteristics: Tall, upright, spreading, vigorous, and bushy. Disease resistant and winter hardy.

Comments: Offspring of 'Peace'; exhibits similar characteristics except for its color.

CHRISTIAN DIOR

Color: Medium red.

Flower Characteristics: Very double blooms have 50 to 60 petals. The lightly scented, cup-shape blooms are borne on long stems. Midseason bloom with fair repeat.

Plant Characteristics: Medium height.

Comments: Petals burn in hot and dry settings, so plant for afternoon shade. An excellent cutting rose because of its fragrance, long stems, and long vase life. All-America Rose Selections (AARS) winner.

CHRYSLER IMPERIAL

Color: Deep red.

Flower Characteristics: Long tapered buds open to 4- to 5-inch double blooms with 40 to 50 petals. Open blooms are full, evenly petaled, with a true rose fragrance. Profuse midseason bloom with good repeat.

Plant Characteristics: Medium, erect, compact, and vigorous. Good in hot weather; prone to mildew.

Comments: Good for small gardens and for cutting. All-America Rose Selections (AARS) winner.

Directory of Roses

DAINTY BESS

Color: Pink.

Flower Characteristics: Long, slender buds open to 5-petaled fragrant blooms. Single petals frame maroon stamens, opening flat to a 4-inch saucer-shape form. Good all-season bloom as a single or cluster.

Plant Characteristics: Medium tall and well branched. Exceptionally winter hardy.

Comments: Climbing form is available. Long-lasting on bush and in bouquets.

DOUBLE DELIGHT

Color: White-yellow with red edge (the red edge deepens in sunlight).

Flower Characteristics: Long, pointed buds open to 5- to 6-inch double blooms with 35 to 45 petals. Well-shaped blooms are scented with a spicy fragrance. Excellent all-season bloom, very free-flowering.

Plant Characteristics: Medium height, upright, spreading, and very bushy.

'Double Delight'

Comments: Use for beds and cut flowers. A popular cutting flower for its color, form, fragrance, and long vase life. All-America Rose Selections (AARS) winner.

FIRST PRIZE

Color: Rosy pink with lighter pink reverse.

Flower Characteristics: Huge buds open to 5- to 6-inch double blooms with 20 to 35 petals. Fragrant and long-stemmed. Good midseason bloom and repeat.

Plant Characteristics: Medium height and vigorous. Needs protection in cold climates.

Comments: A climbing type is available. A good cut flower. All-America Rose Selections (AARS) winner.

GARDEN PARTY

Color: Creamy white with light lavender pink edge.

Flower Characteristics: Large buds open to 5-inch double blooms with 25 to 30 petals. Cup-shape flowers are lightly scented and have large, flaring petals. Profuse midseason bloom with good repeat.

Plant Characteristics: Tall, vigorous, strong, and bushy. Prone to mildew.

Comments: Plant in groups of three or more for dramatic effect. All-America Rose Selections (AARS) winner.

HONOR

Color: Pure white.

Flower Characteristics: Long, pointed buds open to large, 4- to 5-inch double blooms with 20 to 22 petals. The loose, lightly fragrant, blooms grow in singles or in clusters borne on long, strong stems. Good all-season bloom.

Plant Characteristics: Tall, upright, vigorous, and well branched. Prone to mildew in late summer and fall; winter hardy.

Comments: An excellent rose for cutting because of its long vase life. All-America Rose Selections (AARS) winner.

KING'S RANSOM

Color: Pure deep yellow.

Flower Characteristics: Long, slender buds open to 5- to 6-inch, double blooms with 35 to 40 petals. The fragrant, cup-shape blooms grow in singles or in clusters and are borne on long, strong stems. Abundance of blooms early in the season with good repeat.

Plant Characteristics: Tall, upright, vigorous, and well branched.

Comments: All-America Rose Selections (AARS) winner.

MISTER LINCOLN

Color: Deep red.

Flower Characteristics: Double, fragrant, cup-shape blooms with 30 to 40 petals. Large flowers are 4 to 6 inches across, have golden stamens, and are borne on long, elegant stems. Good all-season bloom with good repeat.

Plant Characteristics: Tall, upright, vigorous, well branched, and healthiest of the dark reds.

Comments: Most popular hybrid tea in the red color range. An excellent cutting rose. All-America Rose Selections (AARS) winner.

OREGOLD

Color: Deep golden yellow.

Flower Characteristics: Large, pointed buds, one to a stem, open to double 5-inch blooms with 35 to 40 petals. Cup-shape blooms exhibit a light, fruity fragrance. Abundant midseason bloom with fair repeat.

Plant Characteristics: Medium tall, upright, well branched, and moderately vigorous. Prone to mildew. Protect in colder climates.

Comments: Good cut flower. All-America Rose Selections (AARS) winner.

PARADISE

Color: Lavender blend, petals edged with red.

Flower Characteristics: Medium buds open to fragrant, 5-inch semidouble blooms with 26 to 30 petals. Good all-season bloom.

Plant Characteristics: Medium height, upright, vigorous, and well branched. Mildew prone. Reasonably hardy.

Comments: All-America Rose Selections (AARS) winner.

PEACE

Color: Yellow, flushed with pink as it matures.

Flower Characteristics: Ovoid buds open to 5- to 6-inch double blooms with 40 to 50 petals. The single blooms exhibit a light fragrance and are borne on strong stems. Good all-season bloom.

Plant Characteristics: Medium tall, upright, vigorous, and branching. Exhibits more vigor than the average bush. Very disease resistant.

Comments: Hybridized in 1937, and given out at a United Nations meeting in 1945, 'Peace' marked the end of the war. The first rose to be named "World's Favorite Rose," it is often referred to as the "Rose of the Century." A climbing form is available. Excellent cutting rose. All-America Rose Selections (AARS) winner.

'Perfect Moment'

PERFECT MOMENT

Color: Yellow edged with red.

Flower Characteristics: Large buds open to lightly fragrant, classic hybrid tea blooms.

Plant Characteristics: Medium height, compact, and bushy. Disease resistant.

Comments: All-America Rose Selections (AARS) winner.

RIO SAMBA

Color: Yellow, turning scarlet as it opens.

Flower Characteristics: Pointed buds open to 5-inch blooms with 25 to 30 petals. The lightly fragrant, medium-size blooms grow one to a stem and sometimes in a cluster.

Plant Characteristics: Tall, vigorous, and slightly spreading. Disease resistant and hardy.

Comments: Great color in the garden; best in cool weather. All-America Rose Selections (AARS) winner.

Directory of Roses

SWEET SURRENDER

Color: Medium pink.

Flower Characteristics: Pointed buds open to 4- to 5-inch double blooms with 40 to 44 petals. Large blooms grow as a single on long, strong stems and open flat. Exhibits a true rose fragrance. Fair all-season bloom.

Plant Characteristics: Tall, upright, compact, and winter hardy.

Comments: An excellent cutting flower. All-America Rose Selections (AARS) winner.

TOUCH OF CLASS

Color: Pink shading to coral.

Flower Characteristics: Long, tapered buds open to large 4- to 5-inch blooms with 30 to 35 petals. The lightly fragrant blooms have a hint of a ruffle to the petals and are borne on long, strong stems.

Plant Characteristics: Tall and upright. Disease resistant and winter hardy.

Comments: A good rose for cutting. All-America Rose Selections (AARS) winner.

TIFFANY

Color: Pink with yellow base.

Flower Characteristics: Slender, pointed buds open to 5-inch semidouble blooms with 25 to 30 petals. Classic hybrid tea form, deeply fragrant, borne on strong stems. Good all-season bloom.

Plant Characteristics: Medium tall, upright, vigorous, and bushy.

Comments: A climbing form is available. Excellent cut rose. All-America Rose Selections (AARS) winner.

TROPICANA

Color: Orange-red.

Flower Characteristics: Large, pointed buds open to double 3- to 6-inch, cup-shape blooms with 30 to 35 petals. Lightly fruit-scented blooms grow as a single, or several in a cluster, on long stems. Excellent all-season bloom. Blooms hold color even in the hottest sun.

Plant Characteristics: Upright, vigorous, and well branched. Disease resistant, except to mildew.

Comments: It was the first fluorescent orange rose. A climbing form is available. Excellent for cutting because of its fragrance, long stems, and long vase life. All-America Rose Selections (AARS) winner.

Grandifloras

GOLD MEDAL

Color: Deep yellow tipped with orange-red.

Flower Characteristics: Large, long-pointed buds open to 3- to 4-inch double blooms with 35 to 40 petals. Blooms with a light fruity fragrance in singles or in clusters. Good all-season show.

Plant Characteristics: Tall, upright, vigorous, and bushy. Disease resistant and hardy.

LOVE

Color: Red with white reverse.

Flower Characteristics: Two-tone buds open to double, cupped blooms with 24 to 30 petals. Classic hybrid tea blooms are lightly fragrant. Continuous bloom throughout the season.

Plant Characteristics: Medium height and upright. All-America Rose Selections (AARS) winner.

QUEEN ELIZABETH

Color: Pure soft pink.

Flower Characteristics: Pointed buds open to 3- to 4-inch double blooms with 30 to 40 petals. Cup-shape blooms are loose and lightly tea scented, borne on long, nearly thornless stems. Midseason bloom with excellent repeat, as a single or in clusters.

Plant Characteristics: Tall and vigorous. Disease resistant.

Comments: Considered the perfect grandiflora. A climbing variety is available. Can be used as a hedge. Excellent cut flower. All-America Rose Selections (AARS) winner.

SOLITUDE

Color: Coral orange with pink tinge and yellow reverse.

Flower Characteristics: Pointed buds open to 4- to 5-inch blooms with 32 to 35 petals. Blooms have a light, spicy scent and petals are scalloped along the edge. Continuous bloom.

Plant Characteristics: Tall, upright, bushy, and hardy.

Comments: All-America Rose Selections (AARS) winner.

SONIA

Color: Light pink.

Flower Characteristics: Classic tall buds open to 4-inch semdouble blooms. Lightly fragrant blooms grow as singles or in clusters on long, graceful stems. Profuse continuous bloom.

Plant Characteristics: Small, upright, and loose.

TOURNAMENT OF ROSES

Color: Two-tone pink

Flower Characteristics: Very double blooms measure 4 inches and grow in abundant clusters. Lightly scented.

Plant Characteristics: Medium tall, upright, and vigorous. Disease resistant and cold hardy. Excellent cut flower because it is both long-lasting and fragrant.

'Tournament of Roses'

Comments: All-America Rose Selections (AARS) winner.

Floribundas

ANGEL FACE

Color: Lavender with ruby blush.

Flower Characteristics: Pointed buds open to 4-inch, cup-shape double blooms with 35 to 40 petals. Fragrant, with ruffled petals and yellow stamens. Blooms as single or in a cluster. Midseason bloom, good repeat.

Plant Characteristics: Medium, upright, bushy, and compact. Disease resistant.

Comments: A climbing form is available. All-America Rose Selections (AARS) winner.

APRICOT NECTAR

Color: Apricot pink fading to yellow center.

Flower Characteristics: Double, 4-inch blooms with 35 petals. Cup-shape blooms bear a fruity scent and grow as a single or in a cluster. Abundant midseason bloom with good repeat.

Plant Characteristics: Tall, upright, vigorous, and slender.

Comments: All-America Rose Selections (AARS) winner.

EUROPEANA

Color: Dark blood red.

Flower Characteristics: Semidouble 3-inch blooms with 15 to 20 petals. Lightly scented, cup-shape blooms grow in large sprays. Abundant midseason bloom with good repeat.

Plant Characteristics: Medium height and spread; compact. Very disease resistant.

Comments: Popular exhibition rose. Excellent rose for cutting because of its long vase life. All-America Rose Selections (AARS) winner.

FASHION

Color: Coral to salmon peach.

Flower Characteristics: Double blooms about 3 inches across with 21 to 24 petals. The classic hybrid tea form is lightly fragrant and blooms as a single or in clusters. Blooms midseason with good repeat.

Plant Characteristics: Medium tall, upright, vigorous, and bushy.

Comments: A highly acclaimed floribunda. All-America Rose Selections (AARS) winner.

FRENCH LACE

Color: Ivory white.

Flower Characteristics: Pointed buds open to 4- to 5-inch double blooms with 30 to 35 petals. Lightly spice-scented blooms are the classic hybrid tea form. Blooms grow in clusters of 6 or more. Good midseason bloom with good repeat.

Plant Characteristics: Medium tall, upright, vigorous, and well branched. Disease resistant and hardy.

Comments: Combines the best of the hybrid tea with the extravagant blooms of the floribunda. All-America Rose Selections (AARS) winner.

ICEBERG

Color: Pure white.

Flower Characteristics: Long, pointed buds open to 2- to 4-inch blooms with 30 petals. Fragrant blooms are saucer shaped with yellow center and grow in loose, medium-size sprays the entire length of the branch. Early to midseason bloom with good repeat. Outer petals develop a faint pink tinge in autumn.

Plant Characteristics: Tall, robust, free-branching, and very vigorous. Disease resistant and winter hardy.

Comments: The whitest floribunda, 'Iceberg' is the top white rose on the market. A recurrent climbing variety is available. Suitable for hedges and for group bedding. Excellent cut flower.

INTRIGUE

Color: Red-purple.

Flower Characteristics: Round buds open to 3-inch double blooms with 20 to 30 petals. Ruffled blooms with the scent of an old garden rose grow in singles or in clusters on long stems. Good midseason bloom with good repeat.

Plant Characteristics: Medium tall, vigorous, and upright. Hardy.

Comments: All-America Rose Selections (AARS) winner.

SWEET INSPIRATION

Color: Pure pink.

Flower Characteristics: Pointed buds open to 3- to 4-inch semidouble blooms with 25 to 30 petals. Lightly scented. Flowers early, with good repeat bloom.

Plant Characteristics: Low to medium height. Hardy and disease-resistant.

Comments: Good for low mass or border planting. Cross of 'Sun Flare' and 'Simplicity.' All-America Rose Selections (AARS) winner.

VOGUE

Color: Coral.

Flower Characteristics: Large 4-inch blooms with 25 petals. Lightly fragrant blooms grow as singles or in a cluster. Good all-season bloom.

Plant Characteristics: Short to medium height, upright, vigorous, and compact.

Comments: All-America Rose Selections (AARS) winner.

Climbers/Ramblers

AMERICA

Color: Coral pink.

Flower Characteristics: Large, pointed buds open to 3- to 4-inch double blooms with 40 to 45 petals. Good midseason bloom with fair repeat.

Plant Characteristics: Upright, Disease resistant and winter hardy. Slow to climb.

Comments: All-America Rose Selections (AARS) winner.

BLAZE

Color: Medium red.

Flower Characteristics: Clustered, cupped blossoms are 2 to 3 inches, semidouble, with 18 to 24 petals. Bloom lasts through the season. Improved form produces clusters of blooms on new and old canes. Lightly fragrant blooms hold their color even in hot sun.

Plant Characteristics: Upright, disease resistant, and winter-hardy climber with 6- to 12-foot canes.

Comments: Abundant bloomer is a good selection for pergolas, pillars, and arches.

CÉCILE BRÜNNER, CL.

Color: Light pink.

Flower Characteristics: Dainty buds open to small, 1½-inch sweetly scented double blooms. Abundant early to midseason bloom lasts several weeks, then sporadic recurrent bloom until frost.

Plant Characteristics: Extremely vigorous climber with canes to 20 feet.

Comments: Good for trellises, arbors, and walls. Fine cutting rose. Nearly a climbing miniature.

GOLDEN SHOWERS

Color: Medium yellow.

Flower Characteristics: Small clusters of 4- to 5-inch semidouble blooms with 25 to 35 petals. Cup-shape blooms are loose. Abundant bloom all season.

Plant Characteristics: Floribunda climber that is upright, disease resistant, bushy, and winter hardy, except in extreme winters. Slow to start, but abundant thereafter.

Comments: Most popular of all yellow climbers. All-America Rose Selections (AARS) winner.

WHITE DAWN

Color: Pure white.

Flower Characteristics: Fragrant double blooms have 35 petals and grow in clusters. Sweet rose fragrance. Camellialike blooms last a long time. Good all-season bloom with good repeat.

Plant Characteristics: Vigorous, winter hardy, disease resistant, and quickly spreads over a large area.

Comments: Excellent border rose.

Miniatures

CHILD'S PLAY

Color: White edged with pink.

Flower Characteristics: Double, 2-inch blooms, one to a stem. Abundant all-season bloom.

Plant Characteristics: Low, compact, well branched, and very disease resistant. Grows 15 to 20 inches high.

Comments: All-America Rose Selections (AARS) winner.

GOOD MORNING AMERICA

Color: Yellow.

Flower Characteristics: Double, classic hybrid tea blooms are fragrant and one to a stem. Petals are tipped with red in bright sunlight.

Plant Characteristics: Upright, disease resistant, and winter hardy. Grows 16 to 24 inches tall and is a fine cutting flower.

ICE QUEEN

Color: White.

Flower Characteristics: Very double blooms are long-lasting.

Plant Characteristics: Disease resistant and winter hardy.

Comments: Grows 12 to 14 inches and is a good choice for beds, borders, and hanging baskets. In cool weather, this rose has a pink tinge.

JULIE ANN

Color: Orange-red.

Flower Characteristics: Double, classic hybrid tea form of blooms are 1½ inches across and have 24 to 30 petals. Blossoms exhibit a strong fragrance. Midseason bloom with good repeat.

Plant Characteristics: Upright, disease resistant, and winter hardy.

Bushy rose grows 10 to 14 inches tall.

Comments: Excellent choice for beds, containers, or indoors.

PARTY GIRL

Color: Apricot flushed with pink.

Flower Characteristics: Double, classic hybrid tea form of blooms measure 1¼ inches across and have 25 petals. Blossoms exhibit a rich, spicy fragrance. Midseason bloom with good repeat.

Plant Characteristics: Bushy, upright, compact, disease resistant, and winter hardy. Grows 12 to 15 inches tall.

Comments: Does well in beds, borders, edgings, and containers, and indoors.

PRIDE 'N' JOY

Color: Orange with yellow reverse.

Flower Characteristics: Shapely buds open to colorful blooms.

Plant Characteristics: Vigorous, compact, and rounded.

Pride ' n' Joy

Comments: This bushy rose grows well in containers. All-America Rose Selections (AARS) winner.

WILLIE WINKIE

Color: Pink.

Flower Characteristics: Double, small, cupped blooms. Profuse continuous bloom.

Plant Characteristics: Small and vigorous.

Old Garden Roses

BLANC DOUBLE DE COUBERT

Color: White.

Flower Characteristics: Semidouble, 18- to 24-petaled, loose blooms measure 2 to 3 inches across. Good early to midseason bloom with all-season repeat. Strong, sweet fragrance.

Plant Characteristics: Upright, disease resistant, and very winter hardy.

Comments: Popular, fast-growing rugosa shrub rose grows 3 to 6 feet tall.

BLUSH NOISETTE

Color: Blush white.

Flower Characteristics: Double, cup-shape, richly fragrant blooms measure 2 inches across with 24 petals. Blooms in clusters midseason with repeat.

Plant Characteristics: Upright, arching, and disease resistant, but not always winter hardy. Grows 5 to 10 feet tall with nearly thornless canes. Use as a climber.

CARDINAL DE RICHELIEU

Color: Purple fading to white.

Flower Characteristics: Double, richly fragrant, loose, cup-shape blooms measure 2½ to 3 inches across with 35 to 45 petals. Blooms midseason; not recurrent.

Plant Characteristics: Upright, compact, disease resistant, and winter hardy. Grows 3 to 4 feet tall and is an excellent garden shrub.

EGLANTINE

Color: Deep pink.

Flower Characteristics: Single, apple-scented blooms. Profuse early spring bloom; not recurrent.

Plant Characteristics: Upright, vigorous, and very winter hardy. Grows 6 to 7 feet tall.

Comments: Produces large hips. Dates before 1551.

LOUISE ODIER

Color: Medium pink.

Flower Characteristics: Intensely fragrant, double blooms have 35 to 45 petals and measure 3½ inches across. Abundant midseason bloom with good repeat. Blooms open to cup-shape, then are flatter, quartered, and full.

Plant Characteristics: Upright, slender, disease resistant, and winter hardy. This bourbon rose grows 4½ to 5½ feet tall.

Comments: A favorite of Victorian gardeners.

MME. ALFRED CARRIERE

Color: White.

Flower Characteristics: Gardenia-shape double blooms have 35 petals and measure 3 to 4 inches across. Midseason bloom with good repeat. Blooms are fragrant and grow in clusters.

Plant Characteristics: Upright, arching, and disease resistant, but not always winter hardy. Thorny canes; grows 8 to 15 feet tall.

Comments: Suitable for arches, pergolas, pillars, and walls, or use as a shrub.

PAUL NEYRON

Color: Medium to deep pink.

Flower Characteristics: Double, full blooms measure 4½ to 5½ inches across with 65 to 75 petals. Midseason bloom with fall repeat. Extremely fragrant.

Plant Characteristics: Upright, arching, disease resistant, and winter hardy. This hybrid perpetual grows 5 to 6 feet tall.

ROSA MUNDI

Color: Pink and white striped.

Flower Characteristics: Three-inch cup-shape semidouble blooms have 18 to 24 petals. Good midseason bloom; not recurrent.

Plant Characteristics: Low, sprawling, compact, disease resistant, and winter hardy.

Shrub/Landscape Roses

ALBA MEIDILAND

Color: White.

Flower Characteristics: Double blooms grow in heavy clusters. Lightly fragrant; continuous bloom all season.

Plant Characteristics: Dense and spreading. A good ground cover or hedge.

FAIR BIANCA

Color: White.

Flower Characteristics: Very double, shallowly cupped blooms are heavily scented. Repeat bloom.

Plant Characteristics: Vigorous and upright, growing 3 to 4 feet tall.

Comments: A David Austin rose that excels in beds or as a hedge.

GERTRUDE JEKYLL

Color: Pink.

Flower Characteristics: Double, full-petaled blooms are heavily

'Gertrude Jekyll'

scented with true damask rose fragrance. Repeat bloom.

Plant Characteristics: Vigorous and upright. Grows 4 to 5 feet tall.

Comments: Excellent in border or hedge.

GRAHAM THOMAS

Color: Yellow.

Flower Characteristics: Very double, cup-shape blooms are strongly tea scented. Old rose look with abundant repeat bloom.

Plant Characteristics: Vigorous, bushy, and upright. This David Austin rose grows 4 to 5 feet tall.

SIMPLICITY

Color: Medium pink.

Flower Characteristics: Double blooms grow in clusters. Abundant all-season bloom.

Plant Characteristics: Vigorous and disease resistant.

Comments: Excellent hedge rose or privacy screen. 'Red Simplicity' and 'White Simplicity' varieties are also available.

'Graham Thomas'

Index